Letts

KS1
Success

Age 5-7

English

Revision
Guide

Helen Cooper

Contents

Reading

Writing

Punctuation

Grammar and Spelling

Learning to read is like cracking a code! When you have cracked it, you can enter the wonderful world of reading.

There are different clues (sometimes called **cues** or **strategies**) that you can use to help you. You may sometimes feel like you are juggling lots of different ideas at once!

How to be a brilliant reader!

Use your **phonic** skills to work words out.

sh-ee-p   w-i-th   p-oi-n-t

Look at the shapes of tricky words.

walk

Cut tricky words into bits you know how to read.

ast- ro- naut

Are there any **pictures**? Look and see if they give you any clues to what's happening in the story.

Read around a tricky word.

The cat sat in the bough of the tree.

Look at the other words. Use them to work out what the tricky word might be.

Reading practice

Read the following passage.

One day the children were playing with their hula-hoops in the garden. Adil could spin a hoop around his waist and another one around his neck at the same time! Ibrahim could hula hoop around his knees. Emily looked sad. Every time she tried to do it, the hoop fell straight down. "I will show you how to do it," said Ava.

Which words did you sound out?

Were there any tricky words?

Which words were hard to work out?

Reading with your child is very important. You can check their progress and notice any areas they need more help with. If your child gets tired or appears to be struggling, take turns reading a bit each. This will help to build your child's confidence.

Parent tip!

Keywords

Cues or **strategies** ➤ Ways of working out how to do something

Phonics ➤ Blending letter sounds together to make words

Picture cues ➤ Using the pictures to help understand the story

Listen up

1

Have a go!

Choose a book that you really like. Read it again. Then tell an adult what happens in the story and say why you like it.

Test yourself

1 What is phonics?

2 What do pictures in stories help you to do?

3 Try reading these tricky words.

because   people   water

4 Think of a word that will fit in this sentence.

The c....... drank its milk and ate its fish.

What is a fiction book?

A **fiction** book is a story book.

- The author makes it up.
- A story has a **plot**.
- It has a beginning, a middle and an end. Read it in order or the story will not make sense.
- There is a **setting** – a city, a forest or maybe a jungle.
- There are **characters**.
- It can have a message – something to teach us. For example, that we should look after our planet or be kind to our friends.

Types of fiction

Fiction can be funny, sad, scary and full of surprises and adventures.

How many of these types of fiction have you read?

- Traditional tales – *The Gingerbread Man*, *Goldilocks and the Three Bears*.
- Fairy stories – *Cinderella* or *Sleeping Beauty*.
- Fables – stories with a lesson such as *The Tortoise and the Hare* by Aesop.
- Plays – these are stories acted out on stage.
- Comics.

Do you have a favourite type of story that you like to read?

Listen up
2

Keywords

Fiction ➤ Writing that is "made up" (comes from the writer's imagination)

Plot ➤ The action and events in the story

Setting ➤ The time and place where the story is set

Character ➤ A person or animal in the story

Blurb ➤ Information about the story given on the back cover of a book

Choosing a book

It can be difficult trying to decide which book to read.

Why not visit the library? There are hundreds of books to choose from and they are all free.

Look at the front cover. Do you like the picture? Does it make you want to read the book?

Now look at the back cover. You can read the **blurb**. This is a short piece of writing that tells you what the story is about. It will help you to decide if you want to read it.

If you like an author, look for their website to find out more about their books.

Story book language

Have you heard or read these words in stories?

Once upon a time…

Long, long ago…

There was once a….

And they all lived happily ever after.

Who's been sitting in my chair?

Who's that trip-trapping over my bridge?

Fee–fi–fo–fum!

Run, run as fast as you can!

Top tip! Read as much as you can. If you've enjoyed a book, look for more books written by the same author.

Have a go! Ask an adult to help you to find some websites that have book reviews. You can use them to find some good books to read.

Test yourself

1 Where would you look for the blurb?

2 What is the setting of a story?

3 What does fiction mean?

What is non-fiction?

Non-fiction writing gives you information and is full of **facts**.

Features of non-fiction

The following are the main features of non-fiction.

- Non-fiction writing does not always have to be read from start to finish (unlike a fiction book). The information can be set out in lots of different ways.
- There are often photographs and diagrams. These may have captions or labels next to them to explain things.
- There may be new topic words that you have not come across.
- A non-fiction book has special pages that can help you to find information more easily, for example the **index** and the **glossary**.

Types of non-fiction

These are all types of non-fiction:
- a leaflet for a place to go for a day out
- a menu
- a poster
- instructions for playing a game or building a model
- information on food packets
- signs
- websites

Keywords

Non-fiction ➤ Writing that is true and not made up

Fact ➤ Something that is true

Encourage your child to help you read information signs. For example, if you are at the swimming pool ask them to read the pool rules. This will help them to become more confident about interpreting information and instructions.

POOL RULES

 DON'T RUN
 NO DIVING
 NO PUSHING
 NO BOMBING
 DON'T SHOUT

 SHOWER BEFORE ENTERING POOL
 USE BATHROOM
 WATCH YOUR CHILDREN
 NO FOOD OR DRINKS
  NO ROUGH PLAY

How to find information in a non-fiction book

A non-fiction book contains lots of information, you just have to know where to find it.

Non-fiction books are split into **sections**. A section may be one or two pages long, or it could be a whole chapter.

Look for **headings** (or titles). They may be a question:

How many types of penguins are there?

Look for **sub-headings** (or sub-titles), in each section as they will help you find information.

| **Emperor Penguins** | **Galapagos Penguins** | **Humboldt Penguins** |

The contents page is at the front of the book. It will show you where to find the main topic areas. For example:

Contents	Page number
Where do penguins live?	pages 2–3
What do penguins look like?	pages 4–5
Penguin feeding habits	pages 6–7
Penguin families	pages 8–9

The **index** is at the back of the book. It is in alphabetical order and will help you to find where to go in the book for more detailed information. For example, if you wanted to know what penguins eat you would look in the index under **e** for **eating habits**. It will tell you exactly which page to look at.

Eating habits 6, 7
Emperor penguins 3, 9–10

Read the **glossary** at the back of the book. This is like a dictionary and is in alphabetical order. It explains what words mean. For example, if you are reading about what penguins eat, you might see the term **krill** but you may not know what it means. Look in the glossary.

krill: small, shrimp-like animals

Have a go! Look at a take-away menu. Can you choose a meal? Can you find out how much it costs? How can you order food?

Test yourself

1. Where in a book will you find the index page?
2. What is a glossary?
3. What information will you find on a contents page?
4. What is a fact?

What is poetry?

Poetry plays with words.

A poet plays with the order of words, makes words up and plays with sounds and patterns of words.

A poet wants you to feel something when you read a poem.

There are lots of different kinds of poem. For example:

- Rhyming poems
- Poems that tell a story
- Poems written in shapes
- Funny poems
- Poems that play with sounds
- Poems that play with rhythm
- Poems that use repetition

Can you think of any other types of poem?

We are going to look at examples of different types of poem over the next four pages.

Rhyming poems

Some poems **rhyme**. You will know lots of rhyming poems, for example nursery rhymes.

> Humpty Dumpty sat on the wall,
> Humpty Dumpty had a great fall,
> All the King's horses and all the King's men
> Couldn't put Humpty together again.

Repeating poems

Some poems repeat words and phrases – this is called **repetition**.

> Autumn leaves
> Brown leaves, orange leaves
> Red leaves, yellow leaves
> Autumn leaves
> Crunchy leaves, dry leaves
> Rotting leaves, falling leaves
> Autumn leaves
> Twisting leaves, twirling leaves
> Floating leaves, falling leaves
> Autumn leaves

Playing with sounds

Some poems play with sounds, for example **tongue twisters**.

> She sells sea shells on the seashore.
> The shells she sells are seashore shells, I'm sure.

Shape poems

Some poems are written in shapes. This helps the poet to illustrate the meaning of the poem.

```
                    A
                   big
                screaming
             dreaming rocket
           roared into the deep
       dark black high night sky
       twisting turning twirling up
       shrieking calling squeaking
    flashing flicking booming crashing
    d    d    d    d    d    d    d    d
    o    o    o    o    o    o    o    o
    w    w    w    w    w    w    w    w
    n    n    n    n    n    n    n    n
```

Choose a poet that you like. Use the Internet to see if you can find a clip of their work being performed. This can help you to understand and enjoy their work even more.

Top tip!

Keywords

Rhyme ➤ Words that have the same sound
Repetition ➤ Words that are repeated over and over again

Have a go!

Find a poem that you like.

Learn it off by heart. Practise saying it out loud. Put lots of expression into your voice and add some actions.

Ask your family to listen to you. Challenge them to learn a poem themselves and have a family poetry session!

Test yourself

1. Think of a string of words to rhyme with band.
2. What is repetition?
3. What is a tongue twister?

Poems with rhythm

Some poems play with **rhythm**.

> The train goes rolling down the track
> Clickety-clack, clickety-clack
> Down to London, there and back
> Clickety-clack, clickety-clack
>
> People travel east and west
> Clickety-clack, clickety-clack
> All directions, home is best
> Clickety-clack, clickety-clack

Funny and story poems

Some poems are **funny**.

> There was a young man from Bengal,
> Who went to a fancy dress ball,
> He decided to risk it,
> And go as a biscuit,
> But a dog ate him up in the hall!

Some poems **tell stories**.

Read a copy of "The Owl and the Pussycat" by Edward Lear. This poem has rhyme in it, but it also tells a story.

Can you find any other poems that tell a story?

Keyword

Rhythm ➤ A strong, repeating pattern of movement or sound

Parent tip!

Arrange a trip to the theatre. There are lots of good children's shows out there! This will help your child to hear and see how spoken language plays with words.

Making a picture with words

Poets try to paint a picture with words. There are lots of ways in which they can do this.

- They use **descriptions**.
- They use different styles of words.
- They use words to help you imagine.

Sometimes the words work together to make special effects, like:

 alliteration  **onomatopoeia**

(You might need to ask an adult to help you to read these big words!)

- **Alliteration** happens when words with the same initial sounds are repeated close together.

I sold a silver spoon,
And a silky swirly skirt.
A slippy shell, a stinky soup,
A stitched-up shiny shirt

Can you make up an alliterative sentence using your name? For example:

Rude Ruby races rapidly.

- **Onomatopoeia** happens when words are used that sound like the things that they are describing.

whizz   whoosh   pop   boom   crash

Do these words make you think about fireworks?

Keyword

Description ➤ Saying or writing what someone or something looks like

Listen up
5

 **Have a go!** Make up a sentence about each person in your family using alliteration. Make them as funny or as silly as you can.

 Test yourself

1. Think of some onomatopoeic words to describe playing in puddles.
2. What is alliteration?
3. Finish these sentences using an alliterative word.
   Silly Sally sells _____.
   Big Barney bites _____.

Comprehension

Comprehension means understanding what you have read.
When you first learnt to read, you had to concentrate hard
to work out each word.
Now that you can read, you are able to understand
and think more about what you are reading.
This means that you are developing your
comprehension skills.

Comprehension skills

At school you will practise **comprehension exercises** with your teacher to
develop your **skills**.

❶ Read the text slowly. Read it again to make sure you have understood
it. If there are any words you can't read, think about what tools you
could use to help.

❷ Read the questions and instructions carefully.
For example, you are reading a book about a family of pandas. The
instruction says "**Tick three phrases that describe what Mummy Panda
looks like**." Make sure that you tick three phrases and not just two.

❸ Look for the key words in each question. These are the words that will
help you to find the answers.
For example, if it says "**Where do the Panda family live?**", try looking for
the word "live" in the text or for any other words that might help like "home".

❹ You do not have to work through the questions in order. If you cannot
work out an answer, leave it and go on to the next question. You can
come back to it later.

❺ Remember that the answers are there! It is not a guessing game.

Keywords

Comprehension ➤ Understanding what you
have read
Comprehension exercises ➤ Exercises that
test your reading and understanding
Phrase ➤ A group of words that together
make sense, but is not a full sentence
For example: beautiful black and white coat

Comprehension practice

Read this passage:

The Panda family lived at number 7, Bamboo Drive. They were a large family – Grandma, Granddad, mummy, daddy and five children. We lived next door at number 5.

I loved Mummy Panda. She had a beautiful black and white coat. She had large black patches around her eyes and ears, black legs and a black band around her shoulders, like a scarf. She always smiled when she saw me and asked me to come around for a bamboo shake and bamboo cake. I was not that keen on bamboo to be honest, but as I always enjoyed going to their house, I would nibble and sip politely while we chatted.

Example question: How many children were there in the family?

Are there any key words that will help you? Did you choose **children** and **family**?

Re-read the passage. Did you find the sentence that contained these words? Did you work out the answer?

Answer: There were five children.

Reading aloud to your child is a fantastic way of developing your child's comprehension skills. It gives them access to texts that are more difficult to read than ones they can choose themselves. It also gives them the opportunity to ask questions.

Ask an adult to buy you a magazine. Choose an article to read. Tell someone three facts you have learned from reading it.

1. What does comprehension mean?
2. What is a key word?
3. What should you do if you cannot answer a question in a comprehension test?

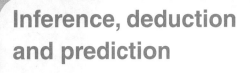

Inference, deduction and prediction

You have already read about **comprehension skills**.
You have learnt how to look for key words in the text and how to use them to find answers.
Sometimes it is not as easy as that.
Sometimes you have to work out the answers from the way the author has used particular words.
Sometimes you will be asked what you think is happening, using ideas from the text or what will happen. You will have to use **prediction** to work this out.
You have to look for clues and use **deduction.**
This is called **inference** or "**reading between the lines**".

Listen up
7

Comprehension practice

Look at this picture and read the text.
Then look at the questions and answers on the next page.

Alex let out a gasp of surprise. Oscar should not have done that!
He felt a surge of annoyance.
He quickly grabbed a reed as well and swung it at his brother.
What a boring, miserable day it had been so far.
They had trudged through the snow for at least half an hour.
The wind was nipping at their fingers, noses and toes.
The ice-packed ground was hard to walk on.
He was freezing. Would they never get home?
He swiped at his brother with the reed. Oscar swiped back.
He swiped at Oscar again. Oscar swiped back.
They both began to jump about.
The red mist began to rise.
Alex began to laugh.
This was a fun game after all. "On guard" he yelled.
The walk didn't seem so bad after all.

Questions

Look at these questions:

1 How does Alex feel when Oscar first swipes him with a reed?

Which words tell you this?

2 How was he feeling before this happened?

How do you know?

3 What time of year do you think it is?

Find two words or phrases that tell you.

4 How do you know that Alex has a change of mood?

5 What do you think will happen next?

Working out your answers

Your answers should be similar to these:

1 Alex felt surprised and annoyed. It says he let out a "gasp of surprise". He felt "a surge of annoyance".

2 He was feeling cross or bored. It says "What a boring, miserable day" and "They had trudged".

3 It is winter. It says "ice-packed ground" and "freezing".

4 It says "Alex began to laugh" and "The red mist began to rise".

5 I think the boys will be friends again and will feel happier walking home.

Were you right?

These are difficult skills for your child to acquire. Share books with your child regularly and ask the types of questions given in the example to develop their understanding.

Parent tip!

Keywords

Prediction ➤ Saying what you think will happen next
Deduction ➤ Working out clues from the text
Inference ➤ Working out the author's hidden meaning

Have a go!

Choose a story that you know well. Re-read it, but this time look out for hidden meanings!

Test yourself

1 What does "reading between the lines" mean?

2 Choose the words and phrases in these sentences that describe Mummy Panda.

She had a beautiful black and white coat. She had large black patches around her eyes and ears, black legs and a black band around her shoulders, like a scarf.

3 Which phrase and words in this sentence tell us that the author did not enjoy eating bamboo?

I was not that keen on bamboo to be honest, but as I always enjoyed going to their house, I would nibble and sip politely while we chatted.

This mind map will help you remember all the main points from this topic. Have a go at drawing your own mind map.

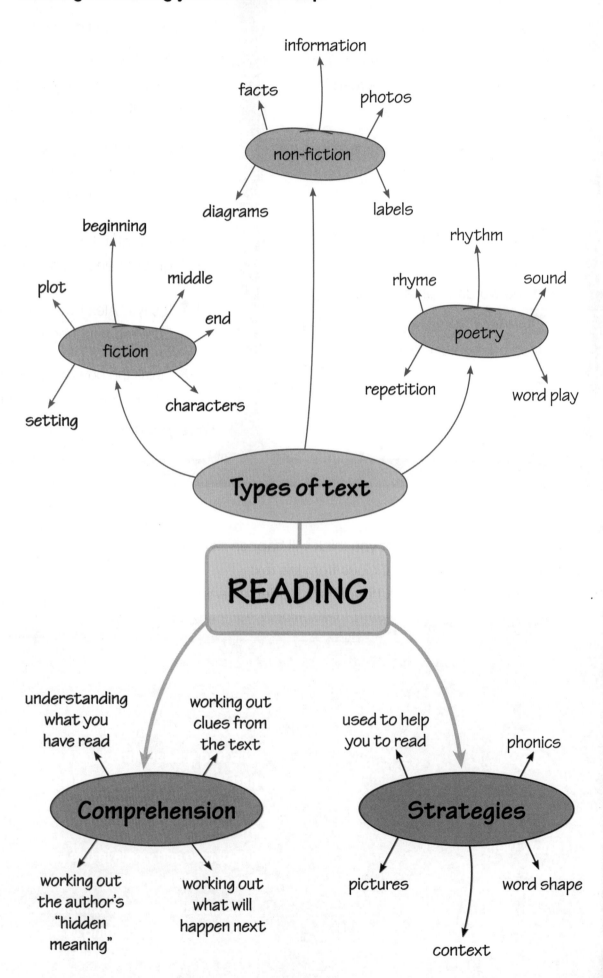

1 Character, setting or plot? Choose the word that describes each phrase.

a. An old man .... **(1 mark)**

b. A forest .... **(1 mark)**

c. Some children get lost in the forest .... **(1 mark)**

d. They are found by a goblin .... **(1 mark)**

e. An underground goblin village .... **(1 mark)**

f. A brave old lady .... **(1 mark)**

2 a. Write a sentence to describe this character: **An old man** **(1 mark)**

....

b. Write a sentence to describe this setting: **A town in winter** **(1 mark)**

....

c. Write a sentence with an idea for a story featuring: **A diamond** **(1 mark)**

....

3 Think of another rhyming word to add to each list.

a. Blink, pink, sink, ... **(1 mark)**

b. Cap, map, flap, ... **(1 mark)**

c. Bed, head, shed, ... **(1 mark)**

d. Might, fight, tight, ... **(1 mark)**

4 Read the text below and then answer the questions.

> Once upon a time there was a group of goblins. Their home was an underground village in a forest. The goblins were harmless and quite helpful, but there was one very strange goblin. His favourite thing to do was to find people who were lost in the wood and offer to help them to find their way out. However, before he would do that, they had to go down into the village and play his favourite game, Hide and Seek.

a. Where did the goblins live? **(1 mark)**

....

b. Which word, which means the same as "odd", describes the goblin? **(1 mark)**

....

c. What do you think would happen to people if they would not play Hide and Seek? **(1 mark)**

....

Handwriting

Your **handwriting** style is important.
Your letters should be:

- formed correctly
- the same size
- in the right place on the writing line
- easy to read

Lower-case letters

Some lower-case letters sit on the line.

a c e i m n o r s u v w x z

Some stand tall on the line.

b d f h k l t

Some hang their tails under the line.

g j p q y

This type of writing is called **print**. Print letters do not join other letters. You can learn them in groups. Each letter starts in the same way.

| coadgq | esf | ijklt | rnmhbp | uy | vwxz |

Print letters are not joined up when you write.

Upper-case letters

Upper-case letters stand on the line.

A B C D E F G H I J K L M N O P Q R S T U V W X Y Z

Upper-case letters are also called capital letters.
Capital letters are not joined up when you write.

Joining letters

You may have started to write **cursive** or joined-up writing.

a b c d e f g h i j k l m n o p q r s

t u v w x y z

Cursive joins

There are four joins:

- **bottom joins** – a letter joins onto the next letter at the bottom
- **top joins** – a letter joins onto the next letter at the top
- **bottom to c shape joins** – the first letter goes up and over to the starting point of the second letter
- **e joins** – joining a letter to e (at the bottom) or joining a letter to e (at the top)

Continuous cursive joins

Each letter has starting and ending lines like this
Write your letters closer together and join them with these lines. You do not need to take your pencil off the paper.

There are only two joins you will need to know:

- top joins go across to the top of the next letter
- top joins to letter e need to curve down

Practise your handwriting regularly, making sure that you form your letters in the correct way. This will help you to develop a good handwriting style.

Top tip!

Keywords

Handwriting ➤ Writing by hand
Print ➤ Writing that is not joined up
Cursive ➤ Writing where lower-case letters are joined up

Have a go!

This sentence has every letter of the alphabet – "The quick brown fox jumps over the lazy dog". Try writing it out in your best cursive writing.

Test yourself

1. Which lower-case letters stand tall on the line?
2. What is another word for upper-case letters?
3. What is the difference between print and cursive writing?

How to use capital letters

Capital letters are used in different ways:

- at the beginning of sentences

  Once upon a time there was a friendly dragon.

- for people's names

  Alfie   Lola   Rueben   Zachary

- for place names

  Lima   Manchester   Morocco   Turkey

- for the days of the week

  Monday Tuesday Wednesday Thursday Friday Saturday Sunday

- for the months of the year

  January   February   March   April   May   June   July   August
  September   October   November   December

- for the names of companies and brands

  Apple   Microsoft   Sony

- for the names of books, films, poems and plays

  The Gruffalo   *The Incredibles*   *Hetty Feather*

- for I when it is a word

  I am going roller skating today.

Sometimes you might hear names of people, places and things like these being called **proper nouns**.

Monday
Tuesday
Wednesday
Thursday
Friday
Saturday
Sunday

Parent tip!

When you are writing with your child, use the capital letter rules yourself! Adults often write entire words in capital letters and write their children's names in capital letters, but this can be very confusing.

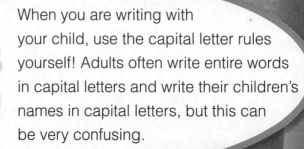

Practice capital letters

Read this passage.

iona and poppy got the bus into stockport. as they walked past a travel agents, they stopped to look at the posters in the window. there were adverts for holidays in australia, florida, mexico and spain. then they went to the book shop. a famous author, ruby redrose, would be signing books there on saturday.

Did you spot that there are no capital letters? Can you use the information on the opposite page to work out how it should be written?

This is how it should be written:

Iona and Poppy got the bus into Stockport. As they walked past a travel agents, they stopped to look at the posters in the window. There were adverts for holidays in Australia, Florida, Mexico and Spain. Then they went to the book shop. A famous author, Ruby Redrose, would be signing books there on Saturday.

Were you right?

Look at this address.

Ms M Contrary,

Silver Bell House,

Cockle Shell Lane,

Prettymaid,

BK2 1RW

The names of the person, the house, the road and the city begin with a capital letter.

Keywords

Capital letters ➤ A capital letter is used at the beginning of a sentence, for names and for I when it is a word
Proper noun ➤ The name of a particular person, place or thing

Listen up 9

Have a go!

You are setting up a secret club. (Shh! Don't tell!) Write the names of all your friends, using a capital letter at the start of each name.

Test yourself

1 Name three different times you would use capital letters.

2 Write down your day and date of birth.

3 Write down the names of four places you would like to visit.

4 Are the capital letters in this sentence correct?

I went to liverpool yesterday with luca.

Writing checklist

When you are writing:

- start a sentence with a capital letter
- leave a space between each word
- write neatly, with your letters correctly formed and a regular size
- use your phonic skills and spelling strategies
- choose the right punctuation mark to finish a sentence

Features of writing

Story writing – a story has the following features:

- characters, a setting and a plot
- a beginning, a middle and an end

Recount writing – this type of writing is written:

- in the past tense
- using time words, for example: **first**, **next**, **after that**, **then**, **finally**
- in the order in which it happened

We went on a trip to Formby beach. The coach was very slow.

First we got lost and drove for miles looking for the right road.

Then we arrived. We carried our bags down to the beach.

I got changed and went into the sea. It was really cold!

Next I had my packed lunch.

After that I built a sandcastle.

Finally we got back on the coach and went back to school.

Listen up
10

Features of writing (continued)

Letter writing – a letter:

- begins Dear ...
- ends either 'love from', 'yours faithfully' or 'yours sincerely'

Dear Emily,
Thank you for my lovely bag.
Red is my favourite colour and I love the sparkles on the strap.
Love from
Olivia

Non-fiction writing – a report has the following features:

- it is written in the present tense
- it uses headings and sub-headings
- it sometimes uses diagrams and photographs

Poetry – a poem might:

- use rhyme or repetition
- play with rhythm and words

Keyword

Recount ➤ A recount retells an event

Top tip!

Reading lots of different types of books will help you with your writing. You will get lots of good ideas and it will help you improve your writing style and spelling.

Have a go!

Try to do lots of different types of writing in a day. You could write a shopping list, send a postcard or organise your toys and make some labels for their boxes.

Test yourself

1. Name a feature of non-fiction writing.
2. How do you begin a letter?
3. Think of a pair of rhyming words that could go in a poem.

Planning your writing

Sometimes you need to **plan** what you are going to write.

If you are making a list or sending a postcard from your holidays, you will not need to write a plan.

However, if you are going to write a story or a report, it is a good idea to set out your ideas before you start.

When you plan your writing:
- say out loud what you are going to write about
- write down ideas and/or key words, including new **vocabulary**
- write down key sentences or phrases
- think about how your ideas might fit in a **sequence**
- use sketches, diagrams and pictures

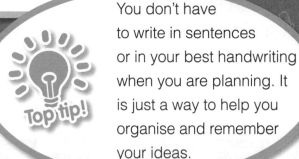

Story writing frames

Look at this **story** writing frame.

Top tip! You don't have to write in sentences or in your best handwriting when you are planning. It is just a way to help you organise and remember your ideas.

Writing a story about Little Bo Peep

Characters	Little Bo Peep – strong, tough shepherdess. Rob and Nick – sheep rustlers, daft, clumsy. PC Ram – local police officer.
Setting	Village, fields, wood.
Plot	Rob and Nick started knitting, need wool, also garden overgrown, sheep lawnmowers.
Intro/build up	See Little Bo Peep with sheep, get idea to kidnap sheep.
Conflict	Follow her to get idea of her movements, battered old blue van.
Resolution	Little Bo Peep has noticed van, she spies on Rob and Nick. Hooks them with her crook, ties them up with her own home spun wool. Agrees to let them join her knitting group if they help her with shearing/spinning.

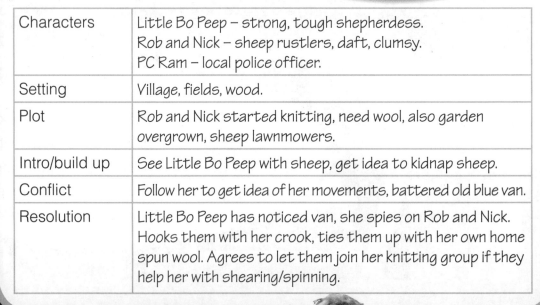

Non-fiction writing frames...

Look at this **non-fiction** writing frame.

Writing about dragons

Title	Facts about dragons.
Sub-headings	What do dragons look like? Where do dragons live? What do dragons eat? What special powers do they have?
Ideas	What do dragons look like? Draw and label a picture of a dragon. Where do dragons live? Photo of a cave. What do dragons eat? Spider diagram. What special powers do they have? List.
Vocabulary	Appearance, diet, habitat.

Checking your writing

Your first attempt at a piece of writing is called a **draft**. When you have finished and read through it, you will probably see things you want to change.

Checklist:
- spend some time looking back over what you have written
- check for spelling, grammar and punctuation mistakes
- check that your writing makes sense
- ask an adult or friend to read through it with you – they may have some ideas about changes you could make
- re write or redraft sections if you want to

Keywords

Plan ➤ To think ahead and note the main ideas

Vocabulary ➤ Words that make up a language

Sequence ➤ The order in which things happen

Draft ➤ A first try at a piece of writing – you might change it or add to it

Have a go!

Why not have a go at a writing project with your friends? Plan and write a film script. Ask an adult if you could use a camera or a tablet to record your film.

Test yourself

1 What is a draft?
2 What is a sequence?
3 Name a type of writing that you may need to write a plan for.

This mind map will help you remember all the main points from this topic. Have a go at drawing your own mind map.

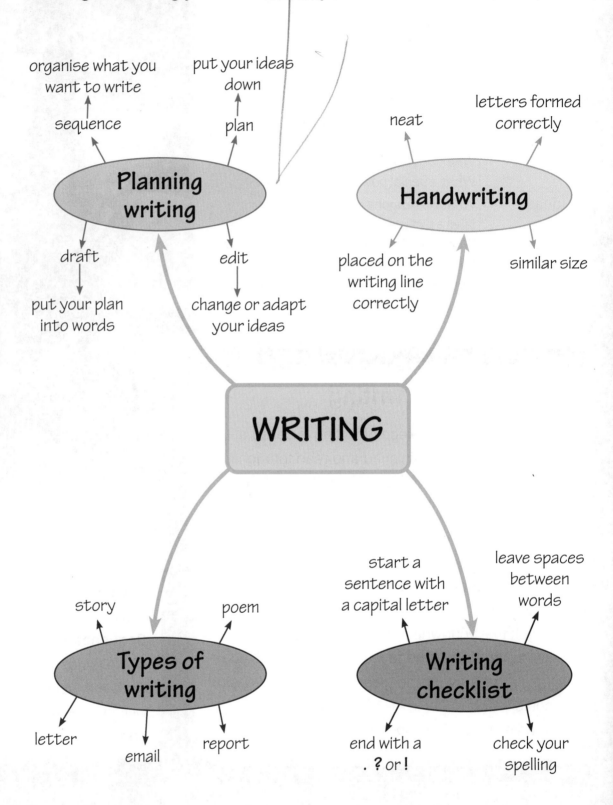

organise what you
want to write

put your ideas
down

sequence

plan

**Planning
writing**

neat

letters formed
correctly

Handwriting

draft

edit

put your plan
into words

change or adapt
your ideas

placed on the
writing line
correctly

similar size

WRITING

story

poem

start a
sentence with
a capital letter

leave spaces
between
words

**Types of
writing**

**Writing
checklist**

letter

report

email

end with a
. ? or !

check your
spelling

1 Rewrite each of the sentences correctly.

a. Iwanttolearntorideahorse. **(1 mark)**

I want to learn to ride a horse

b. my dad says it is an expensive hobby. **(1 mark)**

....

c. How long does it take to learn **(1 mark)**

....

2 Write out each lower-case letter of the alphabet, placing it correctly
on the line. **(1 mark)**

_____

_____

_____

3 **a.** <u>Underline</u> any words that you would find in fiction writing. **(3 marks)**

character **subheading** **setting** **report** **diagram** **plot**

b. (Circle) any words that you would find in non-fiction writing. **(3 marks)**

character **subheading** **setting** **report** **diagram** **plot**

4 Number these notes 1, 2, 3, 4 and 5 to put them in order for a story.
The first one has been done for you. **(4 marks)**

| 5 | The troll falls into the river. |

| 4 | Great Big Billy Goat Gruff butts the troll. |

| 1 | Once upon a time, there were three hungry goats. |

| 3 | Medium-sized Billy Goat Gruff meets the troll. |

| 2 | Little Billy Goat Gruff crosses over the bridge. |

Punctuation marks at the end of sentences

Full stops, **question marks** and **exclamation marks** are **punctuation marks**.
You can use them to finish sentences.
You use them for different types of sentence.

Which one should you choose?

A **full stop** looks like this: ●
It ends a sentence.

> The girl hurried down the hill**.**
> She ran faster and faster and faster**.**

A **question mark** looks like this: **?**
It ends a sentence that asks a question.

> Where was she going**?**
> Who was she running from**?**

An **exclamation mark** looks like this: **!**
It ends a sentence that says something funny, scary, surprising, loud or angry.

> A terrible growl rang out**!**
> A big brown bear was galloping down the hill behind her**!**

It also comes at the end of a command.

> Help me**!**

Stop!

Stop at the full stop. A full stop finishes a sentence. It also reminds you to pause before you read on.

Read these sentences aloud. Don't forget to pause!

> Once upon a time there was a boy called Jack. He lived with his mother.

Listen up
12

Question Time

Who? What? Why? When? Where? How? Which?

These words start questions.

> Who is that?

> What are they doing?

> Why are they doing that?

Write some questions using the other question words – when, where, how and which.

What a surprise!

An exclamation mark can help to make your writing come alive!

> Wow! That's amazing! I love it!

Children sometimes use exclamation marks too much in their writing. Encourage your child to choose the most appropriate punctuation mark to finish a sentence and to reserve the exclamation marks for the most exciting bit.

Keywords

Full stop ➤ A full stop ends a sentence

Question mark ➤ A question mark ends a sentence that asks a question

Exclamation mark ➤ An exclamation mark ends a sentence that shows strong feelings

Punctuation marks ➤ You can use these to make your writing clear and easy to understand – they can also show where sentences start and finish

Have a go!

Think of a different sound and action for each punctuation mark. Make a set of cards with one of the punctuation marks written on each card. Shuffle the cards and put them in a pile. Take turns turning over the cards with a partner. Make the sound and do the action every time you turn over the card. The person who is quickest gets the card!

Test yourself

1 Explain how to use a full stop.

2 What does a question mark look like? Draw one in the air.

3 When do you use an exclamation mark?

4 What should go at the end of this sentence?

Jisoo had the most amazing holiday ever

What do sentences do?

A **sentence** can do lots of different jobs.

- It can ask you a question.

  > Would you like to go ice-skating?

- It can tell you to do something. This is called a **command** or instruction.

  > Put your ice-skates on.

- It can tell you something. This is called a **statement**.

  > I can skate really fast.

- It can show excitement. This is called an **exclamation**.

  > That was a brilliant spin!

What makes a sentence?

Listen up 13

A sentence starts with a capital letter. It ends with a full stop, an exclamation mark or a question mark.

Look at these examples:

> It is really cold in here.

> I nearly fell over!

> How good a skater are you?

A sentence has a verb in it. A verb is sometimes called a doing word. A verb gives a name to an action.

Look at these examples:

> The children **skated** around the rink.

> They **slipped** and **slid** around.

> They **drank** some hot chocolate to warm up.

Types of sentence

Sentences can be different lengths and contain a different number of clauses.

This sentence is short and has one idea or **clause**.

> The dog chased the cat.

This sentence is longer and has two ideas or clauses.

> The dog chased the cat **but** the cat ran up a tree.

The clauses are linked by a joining word (or **conjunction**).

Clause 1 The dog chased the cat.   **Clause 2** The cat ran up the tree.

Keywords

Command ➤ This type of sentence gives an order or instruction

Statement ➤ This type of sentence tells you something that has happened

Top tip! Your writing will be more interesting if you try to use different types of sentence.

Have a go!

Have a look in a cookery book. Can you see how recipes use a lot of commands?

> Put some flour in a bowl. Crack two eggs into a cup.

Why not ask an adult if you can do some cooking?

Test yourself

❶ **What kind of sentence is this?**

> Put your coat on.

❷ **Which punctuation mark should you put at the end of this sentence?**

> Do you have a scarf

❸ **What is missing from this sentence?**

> It was the best time ever

What is a comma?

A **comma** is a **punctuation mark**.

Commas separate items in a list.

Commas make a list clearer and easier to read.

How to use commas in a list

Look at this list:

> red green yellow and blue

Now look at it again and see how the commas make it easier to read:

> red, green, yellow and blue

Look at this sentence:

> I will put cheese tomato cucumber and butter on my sandwich.

Now look at it with commas in place.

> I will put cheese, tomato, cucumber and butter on my sandwich.

Can you see the commas? Can you see that they separate the items in the list? Which sentence is easiest to read?

Always use '**and**' to separate the last two items in the list. You do not need a comma before **and** at the end of the list.

> I like peas, potatoes, parsnip **and** pizza.

> I have a brother, a sister **and** a cat.

> Four children are lining up. Their names are Jack, Conroy, Layla **and** Jacob.

Finding commas

Read this passage and look at how commas are used.

> My mum sent me to the shop. I had to get pasta, bread, peppers and oil. On the way I met Sam, Jamil, Tom and Monika. They asked me to go to the park with them. They were going to play football, basketball or handball.

Look at this list.

> bucket   spade   beach ball   towel

The list can be written into a sentence using commas.

> I took a bucket, a spade, a beach ball and a towel to the seaside.

Keyword

Comma ➤ A comma is a punctuation mark that can be used to separate things in a list

Parent tip!

A comma can be also used to show a break or a pause in a sentence. Help your child to find some examples of these in a newspaper or magazine.

Have a go!

Practise writing some commas. First, write a dot, then add a hook that points to the left: **,**
Write them in different colours. Write some big ones. Write some small ones. Ask someone which one they think is your best!

Test yourself

❶ Circle all the commas in this list:
   A hat, a scarf, some gloves and some boots.

❷ Add the missing commas to this sentence:
   My sister has a book a pen some paper and a pencil in her bag

❸ Write a sentence using this list:
   a car   a bus   a train   an aeroplane

❹ Are all the commas in this sentence in the correct places?
   I can, hop skip jump, and run.

Apostrophes

An **apostrophe** is a punctuation mark.

It can be used to shorten words.

The apostrophe shows where letters have been missed out of a word. This type of word is a **contraction**.

Keywords

Apostrophe ➤
A punctuation mark
Contraction ➤ Two words joined together with letters missing – an apostrophe takes the place of the missing letters

Using contractions

People speak and write using different styles of English.

People often use **contractions** when they chat.

Look at these examples:

"I'm going to the shop."   instead of   "I am going to the shop."

"We're having ice-creams."   instead of   "We are having ice-creams."

"They're having fun!"   instead of   "They are having fun!"

Contractions are often used in messages, postcards or emails.

Look at these examples:

I've gone to the park. I'll be back soon.

Having a lovely holiday. Wish you and Lucy had come with us. She'd have loved the water park!

Can't get to the swimming club tonight.

Can you work out how they would be written without contractions?

Top tip!

Do you know the difference between its and it's?

It's = It is   It's a lovely day = It is a lovely day.
In this case you use an apostrophe because It's = It is
but   The lion opened its big mouth.   In this case you don't use an apostrophe because **its** does not mean "it is".

Forming contractions

In these examples two words are joined together. The apostrophe takes the place of a letter.

did not	didn't
I am	I'm
has not	hasn't
they are	they're
could not	couldn't
cannot	can't

In these examples two words are joined together. The apostrophe takes the place of more than one letter.

I will	I'll
she would	she'd
will not	won't

Try to think of some more.

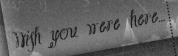

Read this postcard.

Dear Lyla,
We're having a fantastic holiday. There's lots to do. I've been swimming every day and we've been out in a glass-bottomed boat. We've built sandcastles every day. Wish you were here!
Love Salma.

Now look at it again.

Dear Lyla,
We are having a fantastic holiday. There is lots to do. I have been swimming every day and we have been out in a glass-bottomed boat. We have built sandcastles every day. Wish you were here!
Love Salma.

What's the difference?
Which one sounds like Salma is speaking to Lyla? Which one do you like best?

Listen up
15

Have a go! Listen to your friends chatting. See if you can count how many times they use contractions in five minutes!

Test yourself

1. What is **shouldn't** short for?
2. How do you say **he had** as a contraction?
3. will + not = ?
4. Change this sentence using a contraction:

    I cannot help you.

An apostrophe's job

As well as shortening words, an apostrophe can also be used to show that something **belongs** to someone or something.

Apostrophes do an important job. They help to make meaning clear when you are reading or writing.

How to use apostrophes for belonging

Learning how to use apostrophes can be very tricky. Lots of adults find it difficult to use them properly.

These rules will help you understand how to use apostrophes with **singular** words or **nouns**.

- When a singular word **does not end with s**, use an apostrophe like this:

> The horse**'s** hoof   the girl**'s** dress

So the rule is: **singular word** + **'s.**

- When a singular word **ends with s**, there are two different ways you can choose:

> Silas**'s** jacket   or   Carys**'** coat

So the rule is **singular word ending in s** + **'s** or **'.**

Learn the apostrophe rules. Do not mix up apostrophes and **plurals**! Plurals often end with an **s** but do not need an apostrophe. Have a look at signs in shops and cafes when you are out. You will see that incorrectly using an apostrophe is a common mistake.

Top tip!

Keywords

Apostrophe ➤ A punctuation mark that can show missing letters or ownership

Noun ➤ The name of someone or something

Plural ➤ Means more than one

Singular ➤ Means one

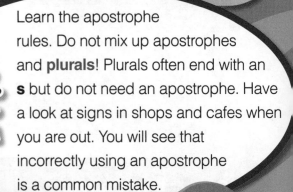

Listen up
16

Charlie's checklist

Charlie is helping with his class assembly. His job is to collect all the props. Have a look at his list below.

> Granny's glasses
> Little Red Riding Hood's cloak
> The woodcutter's axe
> The big bad wolf's sharp teeth

Look at where Charlie has written the apostrophes – are they in the right places?

For example:

- Who has glasses? Charlie has written Granny then has added 's.
  ✓ He is right.

Has he done the same for all the other characters on his list?

Shola's shopping

Shola is shopping for things she has seen at her friends' houses. She has made a list to remind herself.

> Jess's jigsaw
> Paris' pen
> Tess's t-shirt
> Angus' aeroplane

Can you see where she has put her apostrophes? Are they all in the right place?

For example:

- Who has a jigsaw? Shola has written Jess then has added 's.
  ✓ She is right.
- Who has a pen? Shola has written Paris then has added '.
  ✓ She is right.

Have a go!

Get some post-it notes and felt-tip pens. Make labels for different places and rooms in your house. Here are some ideas: *Mum's room, Dad's room, the cat's basket.*

Test yourself

1. Where should the apostrophe go in this sentence?

   I found Alis key on the floor.

2. Is this apostrophe in the correct place?

   I like looking at Ailsas photo's.

3. Add the apostrophes to these phrases:

   the rats tail

   the books page

   the sharks teeth

This mind map will help you remember all the main points from this topic. Have a go at drawing your own mind map.

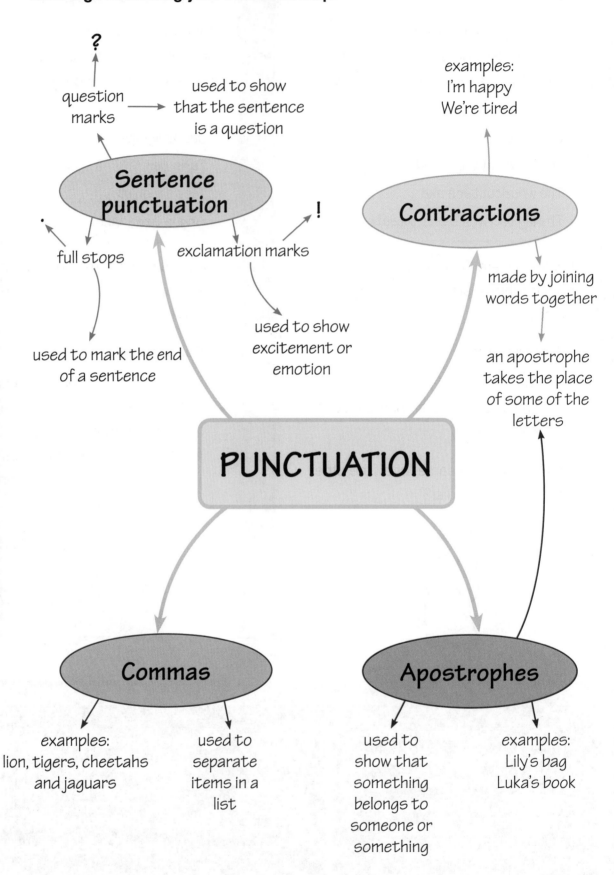

?

question marks → used to show that the sentence is a question

Sentence punctuation

full stops

exclamation marks

!

used to mark the end of a sentence

used to show excitement or emotion

PUNCTUATION

examples: I'm happy We're tired

Contractions

made by joining words together

an apostrophe takes the place of some of the letters

Commas

examples: lion, tigers, cheetahs and jaguars

used to separate items in a list

Apostrophes

used to show that something belongs to someone or something

examples: Lily's bag Luka's book

1 Draw a line to match the punctuation mark to each sentence. **(3 marks)**

| What time does the concert start |

| I'm so excited, I can't wait |

| We are going there in a taxi |

.

?

!

2 Write these sentences again, but change the words in **bold** to contractions. **(5 marks)**

I am going to the concert with my cousins. When **we have** seen the band, **we are** going to a restaurant for pizza. **We would** love to meet the band, but **I do not** think that will happen.

....

....

....

....

....

3 Put the commas into this list. **(4 marks)**

My bag is full. I've put a pen my autograph book some tissues some money a drink and a sandwich in it.

4 Put the apostrophes in the correct place.

a. Where is my cousins bag? **(1 mark)**

b. I want the singers autograph. **(1 mark)**

5 Rewrite the following sentences putting in the missing punctuation.

a. Every school holiday we go to our grandmas house in the country **(2 marks)**

....

b. Were really excited about going **(2 marks)**

....

c. Cant you remember visiting us there **(2 marks)**

....

d. We will take granddads birthday present with us **(2 marks)**

....

What are conjunctions?

Conjunctions are words that join words or parts of sentences. You might also hear them called **connectives**. Here are some common conjunctions:

| and | but | or | because | if | that | when |

Can you think of some sentences using these conjunctions?

Sentences with conjunctions

Read these sentences.

> The girls went climbing every Saturday. They loved it. It was hard. They were getting stronger. They were beginning to find it easier. They always wore trainers. They were the most comfortable shoes. The girls were climbing. Mum sat and read a book.

Now read the same sentences, joined with conjunctions.

> The girls went climbing every Saturday **and** they loved it. It was hard **but** they were getting stronger, **so** they were beginning to find it easier. They always wore trainers **because** they were the most comfortable shoes. **While** the girls were climbing, mum sat and read a book.

Can you see how the conjunctions link the ideas together? They make the sentences easier to read because the words flow together better.

Types of conjunctions

You might have heard about co-ordinating and subordinating conjunctions. These are tricky words and tricky ideas for you to think about!

A **co-ordinating conjunction** joins together words and phrases that are of equal importance in a sentence.

> The girls went climbing every Saturday **and** they loved it.

A **subordinating conjunction** joins together words and phrases where one idea is not as important as the other.

> The girls went climbing every Saturday **because** they loved it.

Types of conjunctions (continued)

Use this table to help you to remember which conjunction is which.

Co-ordinating conjunctions	Subordinating conjunctions
and	when
or	if
but	that
	because

Look at examples of how they are used in these sentences:

Don't worry if your child does not fully understand the different types of conjunction. The important thing is that they understand what conjunctions are and how to use them.

Parent tip!

Co-ordinating Conjunctions

I go to the library every Saturday **and** I choose new books to read.

I enjoy doing this **or** sometimes I go to the park.

I try to do both **but** my mum always says I have to go shopping with her as well.

Subordinating Conjunctions

He cleared the leaves from the path **so** we didn't slip.

We had to leave early **because** my brother was ill.

She could have done better in the exams **if** she had worked harder.

It was a big problem **that** my sister arrived late for school.

Can you think of any more conjunctions? What kind of conjunctions are they?

Keywords

Conjunction ➤ Joins together a group of words or phrases

Connective ➤ You might hear this word being used instead of conjunction

Have a go! Choose a book or a magazine. Read a page or an article and see if you can find the conjunctions that the author has used.

Test yourself

❶ Which conjunction could fit into this sentence?

Iona does not like to do homework _____ she would rather be playing.

❷ Which words are the conjunctions in this sentence?

Every Saturday we go shopping and we go to a cafe because my mum likes to have a coffee.

Language rules

Languages are made up of lots of different words. There are rules that organise these words. The rules are called **grammar**.

You might have heard of these words: **noun**, **adjective**, **verb** and **adverb**. They all do different jobs in sentences.

Nouns

A **noun** is a naming word.

| a rake | a spade | a trowel | a boy |

| a girl | a man | a woman |

A **proper noun** names a particular person, place or thing.

| Finlay | Friday | France |

Adjectives

You can add an adjective to a noun to say more about it. It goes before the noun.

an **angry** man

a **green** bean

a **bendy** carrot

Top tip! Adjectives and adverbs can make your writing more interesting. Try to use them.

Keywords

Grammar ➤ Rules that explain how to organise a language

Noun ➤ A word that names someone or something

Adjective ➤ A word that says more about a noun

Verb ➤ A word for doing or being

Adverb ➤ A word that says more about a verb

Listen up 18

Verbs

A verb is a word for doing or being: for example, to run, to sing, to be. It names the action in a sentence.

A sentence should have a verb.

> I **work** in my garden every day. I **grow** vegetables. I **am** tired.

Can you pick out the verbs in these sentences?

> I see a star. The weather is cold.

Did you pick out **see** and **is**?

Adverbs

An **adverb** says more about a verb.
Adverbs often end in **ly**, for example, quick**ly**, slow**ly**.

Can you find the adverbs in the following example?

> The enormous bean plant curled **tightly** around the garden pole, gripping it **firmly**.

> **firmly** – how it was gripped.

> **tightly** – how the bean plant was curled.

Look in a newspaper or magazine. Use felt-tip pens or highlighter pens to mark nouns, adjectives, adverbs and verbs. Choose a different colour for each type of word.

❶ Think of four adjectives to use with *plant*.

❷ Which adverbs could you use with the verb *grew*?

❸ What type of noun is Spain?

❹ Think of two verbs to put into this sentence.

> We _____ the potatoes that we had_____ in our garden.

Phrases

You know what a noun is.

You know what an adjective is.

You may have heard of **phrases**.

A **phrase** is a group of words that work together. It is not a whole sentence.

What is a noun phrase?

The noun is the main word in a **noun phrase**.
For example:

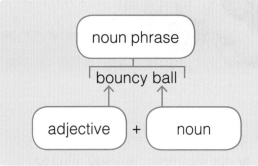

```
              noun phrase
              ┌──────────┐
               bouncy ball
                ↑        ↑
   ┌──────────┐   +   ┌──────────┐
   │ adjective │      │   noun   │
   └──────────┘       └──────────┘
```

Together the adjective and noun make a noun phrase.

You may have heard of an **expanded noun phrase**.

An expanded noun phrase describes and explains in more detail.

> The big bouncy ball bopped Ben on the head.

Listen up

19

Keywords

Phrase ➤ A phrase is a group of words that work together, but not a whole sentence

Noun phrase ➤ A phrase that has a noun as its main word

Noun phrase practice

Find the noun phrases in this paragraph.

The tall man was the goalkeeper. He wore a yellow, shiny jumper and some big, padded gloves. He bounced the ball a few times then kicked it down the field. It was the second ball he had kicked. The first ball was the ball that bounced into the crowd and bopped Ben on the head. Ben had to go to First Aid. Now Ben has a sore head.

Did you find all the noun phrases?

tall man, yellow shiny jumper, big padded gloves, the ball that bounced into the crowd, sore head

Parent tip! Your child will need to understand what a noun is, what an adjective is and how commas work in lists in order to understand noun phrases.

Have a go! Play the game "*I went to the supermarket.*" with your friends. The person who goes first chooses an item they have bought at the supermarket and everyone else adds an adjective.

Example: "I went to the supermarket and I bought some cheese. I went to the supermarket and I bought some blue cheese. I went to the supermarket and I bought some smelly blue cheese."

Test yourself

1. What is a noun phrase?
2. Read this noun phrase: a little bag
   a. Which word is the adjective?
   b. Which word is the noun?
3. Put these words together to make a noun phrase:
   chair soft big the

We have already learnt that a **verb** is a word for doing or being. All sentences have a verb.

The **tense** of the verb in a sentence tells you when something happens.

There are lots of irregular verbs. Encourage your child to read as much as possible. This is a great way for them to be made aware of verb forms in context.

The present tense

The **present** tense is about something that is happening now.

The fish **swims** quickly.

The seaweed **moves** gently with the waves.

Sometimes you use the **present** tense like this:

The shark is **swimming**.

The fish are **feeding** around the coral reef.

Keywords

Present ➤ Something that is happening now

Past ➤ Something that has happened

The past tense

The **past** tense is about something that has already happened.
To change most verbs to the past tense, add **ed**.

wave | The octopus **waved** its tentacles.

scuttle | The crab **scuttled** under a rock.

Sometimes you use the past tense like this:

> The ray **was moving** quickly through the water. The sea lions **were playing** around the rocks.

You will use the verb **to be** a lot. This is how it changes in the present tense and the past tense:

Present	I am	he is	she is	we are	you are	they are
Past	I was	he was	she was	we were	you were	they were

You will also use the verb **to go** a lot. This is how it changes:

Present	I go	he goes	she goes	we go	you go	they go
Past	I went	he went	she went	we went	you went	they went

Have a go!

Look at this poem "Then and now":

When I was young I crawled

Now I walk

When I was young I slept in a cot

Now I sleep in a bed

When I was young I ate baby food

Now I munch vegetables

Try adding some more lines.

Test yourself

1 Which tense are these verbs?

   swims floats paddles

2 Which tense are these verbs?

   floated   paddled

3 Change these to the past tense:

   I am   They are going

   May is watching

4 Finish this sentence.

   Yesterday they _____ sailing.

What is a suffix?

A **suffix** is a group of letters that is added to the end of the word. When you add a suffix to a word you make a new word.

A suffix can change the **word class** of a word.

Common suffixes

These are all common suffixes:

- **–ed**
- **–ing**
- **–ly**
- **–er**
- **–est**

–ed will help you to form verbs in the past tense

> I **lived** in a little village.
> I **copied** my friend's answers!

–ing will also help you to form verbs in the past and present tense

> I am **writing**.
> You were **singing**.

–ly will help you to form adverbs

> **quickly**   **slowly**

–er means more and **–est** means most. Look what happens when you add **–er** and **–est**:

> Isabelle cycled **fast**.
> Jonah cycled **faster**.
> Pasha cycled **fastest**.

Meanings

–ness is a word for a feeling or a way of being

- sad – **sadness**
- happy – **happiness**
- shy – **shyness**

> Nina's smile showed her happi**ness** when she won the race.

–ful means full

- help – **helpful** (full of help)
- hope – **hopeful** (full of hope)

> She was hope**ful** that she would win again the next time!

Keywords

Suffix ➤ A group of letters that is added to a word to change its meaning

Word class ➤ The grammar group that a word belongs to, for example a noun, an adjective, an adverb or a verb

Spelling rules

English can be tricky. Here are some spelling rules that will help you, but remember that there are always some words that will break these rules!

- If you add **–er** or **–est** to a word that ends in a single vowel and consonant, double the consonant before adding the suffix.

  > **fat**   fat + t + er = fatter
  > **thin**   thin + n + est = thinnest

- If you add **–er** or **–est** or **–ly** to a word that ends with **–y**, take off the **–y** and add an **–i** before adding the suffix.

  > **happy**
  > happy + i + er = happier
  > happy + i + est = happiest
  > happy + i + ly = happily

- If you add **–ing** to a word that ends in **–e**, take off the **–e** before adding **–ing**.

  > drive   drive + ing = driving
  > ride   ride + ing = riding

- If you add **–ful** to a word, it only needs one **–l**, not two, e.g.

  > care + ful = careful ✓
  > care + full = carefull ✗

Have a go!

There are lots of games that you can play online to help improve your spelling and find out more about suffixes. Ask an adult to find some with you.

Test yourself

❶ What word would you make if you added the suffix *–less* to the word hope?

❷ What is wrong with this word – "rideing"?

❸ a. Add *–ly* to these two words:

   soft_____   smooth_____

   b. Now make up a sentence for each of these words.

What is a homophone?

Homophones are words that sound the same.
They do not mean the same thing or have
the same spelling.
Be careful! It is easy to get them mixed up.

a pair of pears

Do you think these homophones have been used correctly?

> Can you **here** me?

> I am sitting **hear**.

What about these ones?

> I don't **no** where I have put my book.

> **Know**, you can't help me.

How can you check?

There / their / they're

Which one should you use?

> They put **their** coats on their pegs.

> **They're** hanging them up.

> **There** are a lot of coats on the pegs.

Remember:

- **they're** is a contraction that means **they are**.

  > **They're** very funny.

- **their** means that something belongs to them (e.g. their coats, their pegs).

  > They are carrying **their** bags.

- **there** means a position or a place.

  > **There** is a mouse in our house.
  > Look over **there**!

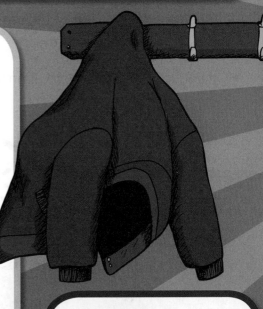

Keywords

Homophone ➤ A word that sounds like another word, but has a different meaning and spelling

Dictionary ➤ A book that explains what a word means, how to spell it and where it comes from

To / too / two

Which one should you use?

I have **two** cats.

I went **to** the park.

I went **too** fast on the roundabout.

Remember:

- **two** means number two.

  He has **two** sisters.

- **to** is a word that can be used with a verb (e.g. to run, to hop, to skip) **or** it can mean going towards (e.g. to the park, to the shop, to the kitchen).

  He wants **to** go **to** the river.

- **too** is used with an adjective or adverb – too big, too slow, too little.

  He is **too** little.

Look at these homophones.

see	sea
bare	bear
sun	son
night	knight
new	knew
for	four
be	bee
read	reed
blue	blew
through	threw
hare	hair
pear	pair
quite	quiet
one	won

Can you think of any other pairs of homophones?

Listen up
22

Top tip! Not sure which homophone to use? Use a **dictionary** to check both spellings and find their meanings.

Have a go! Make a card game to play with a friend. Have two piles of cards. *Homophones* written on one pile, *definitions* on the other. Match homophones to definitions as quickly as you can to be the winner!

Test yourself

❶ What is a homophone?

❷ Write a homophone for hair.

❸ Finish this list of homophones: there, they're, _____

❹ Which homophone would you put in this sentence?

My food is_____ hot.

Choose from to, too or two.

Grammar and Spelling

This mind map will help you remember all the main points from this topic. Have a go at drawing your own mind map.

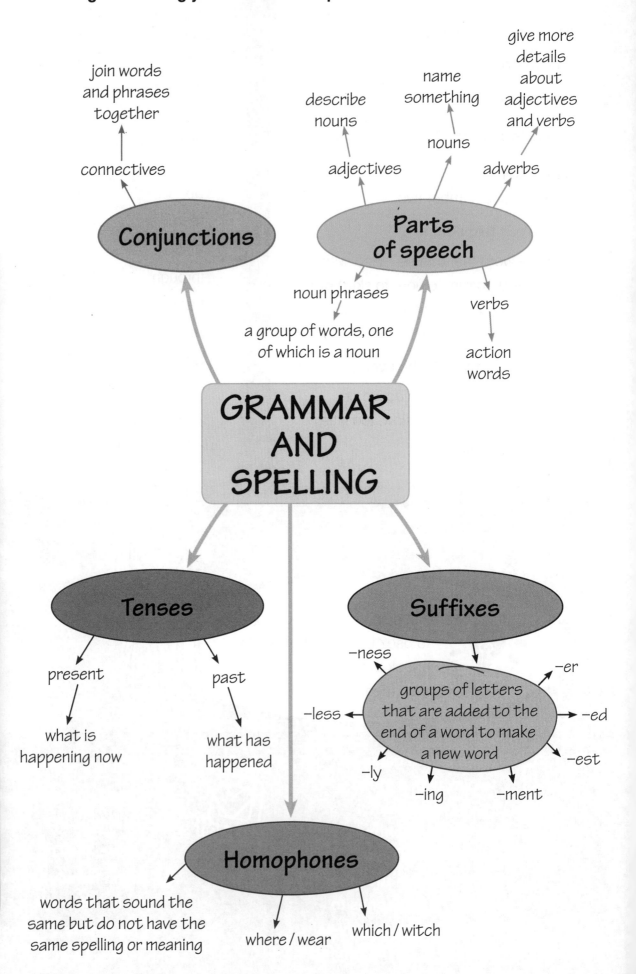

join words and phrases together

connectives

Conjunctions

describe nouns

name something

give more details about adjectives and verbs

adjectives

nouns

adverbs

Parts of speech

noun phrases

a group of words, one of which is a noun

verbs

action words

GRAMMAR AND SPELLING

Tenses

present

what is happening now

past

what has happened

Suffixes

–ness

–less

groups of letters that are added to the end of a word to make a new word

–er

–ed

–est

–ly

–ing

–ment

Homophones

words that sound the same but do not have the same spelling or meaning

where / wear

which / witch

1 For each sentence below, (circle) the correct verb tense.

   a. Every Saturday we go to the library.   **past/present**   **(1 mark)**

   b. Last Sunday we went to the cinema.   **past/present**   **(1 mark)**

   c. I am in a drama group.   **past/present**   **(1 mark)**

   d. I was in a swimming club.   **past/present**   **(1 mark)**

2 Write the correct homophone for each sentence.

   a. pear or pair?   My sister has a new .... of shoes.   **(1 mark)**

   b. we're/where?   I am not sure .... to put this book.   **(1 mark)**

   c. blew/blue?   The wind .... the leaves off the trees.   **(1 mark)**

3 Choose a suitable conjunction from the box below to complete each sentence.

> **and   but   or   so   after   although   because   if   that   when   while**

   a. We were on our way to my grandma's house .... our car
   ran out of petrol.   **(1 mark)**

   b. My mum was so cross .... she hadn't noticed the tank
   was nearly empty.   **(1 mark)**

   c. My little sister started to cry because she was hungry, ...
   then she remembered we had some biscuits.   **(1 mark)**

4 Choose a suitable suffix from the box below to complete each sentence.

> **er   est   ed   ing   ful   less   ly   ment   ness**

   a. It was care...*less*... to forget about the appointment.   **(1 mark)**

   b. It would be quick...*er*... to walk.   **(1 mark)**

   c. My dad and brother had an argu...*ment*...   **(1 mark)**

   d. I like to be help...*ful*... if I can.   **(1 mark)**

1 Look at the sentences below.
The **capital letters** and **full stops** are missing.

   a. **Write** a full stop in each correct place. **(2 marks)**

   b. Circle **three** words that need a capital letter. **(2 marks)**

sara and caleb are playing hopscotch in the playground. they have written the numbers with a piece of chalk.

2 Tick the punctuation mark that should complete each sentence. **(3 marks)**

Sentence	Full stop	Exclamation mark	Question mark
Where are you going			
It was amazing			
I saw a rabbit in a field			

3 Draw lines to match each sentence with its correct type. **(1 mark)**
The first one has been done for you.

Put your coat on.   Command

Hurry up!   Question

Do you want to go to the park?   Statement

It's cold outside.   Exclamation

4 In the table, write in full each of the words with an apostrophe.
The first one has been done for you. **(2 marks)**

Word with an apostrophe	Words in full
I've	I have
We'll	
He's	

5 **a.** Tick the two sentences that are correct. **(1 mark)**

    Mum and dad went to the gym yesterday.   ☐

    Dad go on an exercise bike.   ☐

    Mum like to swim.   ☐

    They had coffee afterwards.   ☐

b. Rewrite the two incorrect sentences, correcting the mistakes.   **(2 marks)**

....

....

6 Look at this picture.

Write a **noun phrase** to describe the hat.   **(1 mark)**

The ...., ... hat.

7 What type of word is **'silently'** in the sentence below?   **(1 mark)**

The fish swam **silently** through the coral.

Tick one:

A noun   ☐

A verb   ☐

An adjective   ☐

An adverb   ☐

8 Write a conjunction (joining word) to complete each sentence.

Today I had a bowl of pasta .... my sister had a risotto.   **(1 mark)**

We wanted to play in the garden .... it was raining.   **(1 mark)**

We decided to watch TV .... it was too wet to play outside.

                                                                          (1 mark)

9 (Circle) the best option to complete the sentence. **(1 mark)**

Elephants are .... than mice.

big   biggest   bigger   most big

10 Tick the best option to complete the sentence. **(1 mark)**

Elephants .... long, ivory tusks.

Tick **one:**

has ☐

are having ☐

will have ☐

have ☐

11 Tick the two sentences that are correct. **(2 marks)**

The other children is going to play in the park. ☐

Dominic is carrying a ball. ☐

I are staying at home. ☐

I am going to go there later. ☐

12 Write the **past tense** of the verb "cook" in the space. **(1 mark)**

I cook pasta for my dinner.

I .... pasta for my dinner.

13 Choose the correct word to complete the sentence.

a. I have a new .... of shoes. **(pair / pear)** **(1 mark)**

b. He is his mother's only .... **(son / sun)** **(1 mark)**

14 Choose the correct suffix to complete each sentence.

> –ly   –ness   –er

a. Please walk careful................ across the slippy floor.   **(1 mark)**

b. The hare ran fast................ than the tortoise.   **(1 mark)**

c. I shared my sweets as an act of kind................   **(1 mark)**

15 What type of word is "noisily" in the sentence below?   **(1 mark)**

The swing creaked **noisily** *as it moved backwards and forwards.*

Tick **one:**

A noun ☐

A verb ☐

An adjective ☐

An adverb ☐

16 Which sentence has the correct punctuation?   **(1 mark)**

Tick **one:**

Polly, put the kettle on. ☐

Polly, put the kettle on ☐

polly, put the kettle on ☐

polly, put the kettle on. ☐

READING

Test yourself

page 5

1 Phonics is blending letter sounds together to make words
2 Pictures help you understand more about a story
3 Ask an adult to help you with these words if needed
4 cat

page 7

1 On the back cover of a book
2 The time and place where a story is set
3 Writing that is made up

page 9

1 At the end of the book
2 A list of words and their meanings
3 It will show you all the main topics covered in the book
4 A fact is something that is known to be true

page 11

1 For example land, sand, hand
2 Repetition is using the same word / phrase / sound over and over
3 A tongue twister is a phrase that uses the same words or sounds that are difficult to pronounce quickly and correctly

page 13

1 For example:
  splash, splosh
2 Words with the same initial sound
3 seashells, biscuit

page 15

1 Comprehension is understanding a text
2 A key word is a word that helps you find the answer to a question
3 Leave it and go onto the next question, and then come back to it later if there is time

page 17

1 "Reading between the lines" means understanding the meaning of a text using clues and ideas
2 "beautiful black and white coat" "large black patches" "black legs" "black band around her shoulders"
3 "not that keen" "nibble and sip politely"

Practice questions

page 19

1 **a.** character **(1 mark)**
  b. setting **(1 mark)**
c. plot **(1 mark)**
d. plot **(1 mark)**
e. setting **(1 mark)**
f. character **(1 mark)**

2 **a.** Accept an answer like the following: "The old man had wrinkles around his bright blue eyes." **(1 mark)**
  b. Accept an answer like the following: "The town glowed white, covered in snow." **(1 mark)**
  c. Accept an answer like the following: "Explorers find a huge diamond in a tomb in the pyramid." **(1 mark)**

3 Accept suitable answers, e.g.
  a. link **(1 mark)**
  b. tap **(1 mark)**
  c. lead **(1 mark)**
  d. sight **(1 mark)**

4 **a.** In an underground village in a forest **(1 mark)**
  b. strange **(1 mark)**
  c. Accept an answer like the following: "The goblin wouldn't help them to find their way out of the wood" or "The goblin would leave them where they were". **(1 mark)**

WRITING

Test yourself

page 21

1 b, d, f, h, k, l, t
2 Upper-case letters are capital letters
3 Cursive writing is joined-up lower-case writing; print writing is not joined up

page 23

1 Accept three suitable answers, e.g. At the start of a sentence; for people's names; for I when it is a word
2 Check your child's answer – the day and month should be written with a capital letter
3 Check your child's answer
4 No – Liverpool and Luca should start with a capital letter

page 25

1 Any answer from – a diagram, a photo, a labelled picture, written in the present tense
2 A letter begins with "Dear..."
3 Accept any pair of rhyming words

page 27

1 A draft is a piece of writing that is being worked on and might have changes made to it

2 A sequence is the order of events in a piece of writing.

3 A story, a report, a poem

Practice questions
page 29

1 a. There are no spaces between the words
   I want to learn to ride a horse (1 mark)

b. A sentence should start with a capital letter
   My dad says it is an expensive hobby. (1 mark)

c. The sentence should end with a question mark
   How long does it take to learn? (1 mark)

2 Check that your child has written all the lower-case
letters of the alphabet correctly (1 mark)

3 a. character (1 mark) setting (1 mark) plot (1 mark)

b. subheading (1 mark) report (1 mark)
diagram (1 mark)

4 1 = Once upon a time there were three hungry goats.
2 = Medium-sized Billy Goat Gruff meets the troll.
3 = Great Big Billy Goat Gruff butts the troll. 4 = The
troll falls into the river. 5 = Little Billy Goat Gruff
crosses over the bridge. (5 marks)

PUNCTUATION

Test yourself
page 31

1 A full stop is used at the end of a sentence

2 Draw a question mark in the air

3 It is used at the end of a sentence that is showing
emotion

4 An exclamation mark or a full stop

page 33

1 Command

2 A question mark

3 An exclamation mark

page 35

1 A hat, a scarf, some gloves and some boots

2 My sister has a book**,** a pen**,** some paper and a pencil
in her bag.

3 Accept a suitable sentence, e.g. A car and a bus are
driven on roads, a train goes on tracks and a plane
flies in the air.

4 No – it should be: I can hop, skip**,** jump and run.

page 37

1 should not

2 he'd

3 won't

4 I can't help you.

page 39

1 Alis' key or Alis's key

2 No – it should be Ailsa's photos

3 the rat's tail, the book's page, the shark's teeth

Practice questions

page 41

1
What time does the concert start   . (1 mark)
I'm so excited, I can't wait   ? (1 mark)
We are going there in a taxi   ! (1 mark)

2 **I'm (1 mark)** going to the concert with my cousins.
When **we've (1 mark)** seen the band, **we're (1 mark)**
going to a restaurant for pizza. **We'd (1 mark)** love
to meet the band, but **I don't (1 mark)** think that will
happen.

3 My bag is full. I've put a pen, **(1 mark)** my autograph
book, **(1 mark)** some tissues, **(1 mark)** some money,
(1 mark) a drink and a sandwich in it.

4 a. cousin's bag (1 mark)
b. singer's autograph (1 mark)

5 a. Every school holiday we go to our grandma's
house in the country. **(2 marks: award 2 marks
for both punctuation marks; only 1 mark for
one punctuation mark)**

b. We're really excited about going! **(2 marks:
award 2 marks for both punctuation marks;
only 1 mark for one punctuation mark)**

c. Can't you remember visiting us there?
**(2 marks: award 2 marks for both
punctuation marks; only 1 mark for one
punctuation mark)**

d. We will take granddad's birthday present
with us. **(2 marks: award 2 marks for both
punctuation marks; only 1 mark for one
punctuation mark)**

GRAMMAR AND SPELLING

Test yourself
page 43

1 because

2 and, because

page 45

1 Accept four suitable adjectives: green, leafy, tall,
sticky

2 Accept suitable adverbs: slowly, quickly

3 A proper noun

4 ate / sold, grown / planted

page 47

1 A noun phrase is a group of words (including a noun)
that work together

2 a. little
b. bag

3 the big, soft chair

Answers

page 49

1 present
2 past
3 I was, They were going, May was watching
4 Accept suitable answer: went/tried/enjoyed

page 51

1 hopeless
2 The "e" should be deleted – "riding"
3 **a.** soft**ly**, smooth**ly**
  b. Accept any two sentences that use these adverbs correctly

page 53

1 Homophones are words that sound the same but have different spellings and meanings
2 hare
3 their
4 too

Practice questions

page 55

1 **a.** (present)   **(1 mark)**
  b. (past)   **(1 mark)**
  c. (present)   **(1 mark)**
  d. (past)   **(1 mark)**

2 **a.** pair   **(1 mark)**
  b. where   **(1 mark)**
  c. blew   **(1 mark)**

3 **a.** when/and/but   **(1 mark)**
  b. because   **(1 mark)**
  c. but   **(1 mark)**

4 **a.** care**less**   **(1 mark)**
  b. quick**er**   **(1 mark)**
  c. argu**ment**   **(1 mark)**
  d. help**ful**   **(1 mark)**

Mixed Practice Questions

page 56–59

1 **a.** Sara and Caleb are playing hopscotch in the playground**.** They have written the numbers with a piece of chalk**. (2 marks)**
  b. (S)ara and (C)aleb are playing hopscotch in the playground.(T)hey have written the numbers with a piece of chalk. **(2 marks if all capital letters identified, 1 mark if only some are identified)**

2

Sentence	Full stop	Exclamation mark	Question mark
Where are you going			✓ **(1 mark)**
It was amazing		✓ **(1 mark)**	
I saw a rabbit in a field	✓ **(1 mark)**		

3 Put your coat on. → Command
  Hurry up! → Question   **(1 mark)**
  Do you want to go to the park? → Statement   **(1 mark)**
  It's cold outside. → Exclamation   **(1 mark)**

4

Word with an apostrophe	Words in full
I've	I **have**
We'll	We will or we shall **(1 mark)**
He's	He is **(1 mark)**

5 **a.** Mum and dad went to the gym yesterday.✓
     They had coffee afterwards.✓   **(1 mark)**
  b. Dad **went** on an exercise bike.   **(1 mark)**
     Mum like**s** to swim.   **(1 mark)**

6 Accept any suitable noun phrase, e.g. the hard, yellow hat.   **(1 mark)**

7 An adverb ✓   **(1 mark)**

8 Possible answers: **and, but**   **(1 mark)**
  Possible answer: **but**   **(1 mark)**
  Possible answer: **because**   **(1 mark)**

9 (bigger)   **(1 mark)**

10 have ✓   **(1 mark)**

11 Dominic is carrying a ball. ✓   **(1 mark)**
  I am going to go there later. ✓   **(1 mark)**

12 I **cooked** pasta for my dinner.   **(1 mark)**

13 **a.** pair   **(1 mark)**   **b.** son   **(1 mark)**

14 **a.** care**fully**   **(1 mark)**
  b. fast**er**   **(1 mark)**
  c. kind**ness**   **(1 mark)**

15 An adverb ✓   **(1 mark)**

16 Polly, put the kettle on. ✓   **(1 mark)**

Glossary

Adjective – A word that says more about a noun

Adverb – A word that says more about a verb

Apostrophe – A punctuation mark used to show that something belongs to someone or something or to shorten words.

Blurb – Information about a story found on the back cover of a book

Capital letters – Upper-case letters, used as a punctuation mark at the beginning of a sentence

Character – A person or animal in a story

Comma – A punctuation mark used in a list

Command – This type of sentence gives an order or instruction

Comprehension – Understanding what you have read

Comprehension exercises – Exercises that test your reading and understanding

Conjunction – Words that join parts of a sentence

Connective – A "joining" word, such as a conjunction

Contraction – A word made from two words that have been shortened using an apostrophe

Cursive – Joined up handwriting

Deduction – Working out clues from a text

Description – Saying or writing what someone or something looks like

Dictionary – A book that explains what words mean

Draft – A first attempt at writing

Exclamation mark – A punctuation mark that shows surprise or excitement

Fact – Something that is true

Fiction – Imaginary or made up story writing

Full stop – A punctuation mark used at the end of a sentence

Grammar – Rules that explain how to organise a language

Handwriting – Writing by hand

Homophone – Words that sound the same but have different spellings and meanings

Inference – Working out the hidden meaning in a piece of writing

Non-fiction – Writing about facts and information that is true

Noun – A word that names a person or thing

Noun phrase – A group of words that work together as a noun. The main word is a noun

Past / Past tense – Something that has happened

Phonics – Using letter sounds to read and spell words.

Phrase – A group of words that work together

Picture cues – Using pictures to help understand what you are reading

Plan – A way to arrange or decide writing ideas

Plot – A plan for a story

Plural – More than one

Prediction – Saying what you think will happen next

Present / Present tense – Something that is happening now

Print – Handwriting that is not joined up

Proper noun – The name of a particular person, place or thing

Punctuation marks – You can use these to make your writing clear and easy to understand – they can also show where sentences start and finish

Glossary

Question mark – A punctuation mark used at the end of a sentence that is a question

Recount – A piece of writing that retells an event

Repetition – Words that are repeated over and over again

Rhyme – Words that have the same sound

Rhythm – A strong, repeating pattern of movement or sound

Sequence – Putting events in chronological order

Setting – The time and place where the story is set

Singular – One

Statement – This type of sentence tells you something that has happened

Strategies – Ways of working something out

Suffix – A group of letters added to the end of a word

Verb – A word for doing or being

Vocabulary – Words that make up a language

Word class – The grammar group that a word belongs to, for example a noun, an adjective, an adverb or a verb

Index